Celebrate Diwali

Deborah Heiligman
Consultant, Dr. Vasudha Narayanan

NATIONAL GEOGRAPHIC
WASHINGTON, D.C.

In Bangalore, India,
children dress as
the monkey god
Lord Hanuman, who
helped Rama
defeat Ravana.

sweets

In autumn, Hindu people all over the world celebrate Diwali. People from Sikh and Jain faiths celebrate Diwali, too. We celebrate with sweets, lights, and fireworks.

We hear stories of great, important battles. Some Hindus tell of Rama, who killed the demon Ravana. When Rama and his wife Sita returned from the war, he was crowned king.

Other Hindus tell the story of Lord Krishna, who killed the demon Narakasura.

lights

Statue of Lord Krishna

fireworks

Light triumphs over darkness.

In each story, we learn about the victory of good over evil, how light triumphs over darkness. Diwali is called the Festival of Lights.

We also tell about Lakshmi, the goddess of wealth. We hope Lakshmi will bring us good fortune.

*During Diwali, Sikhs light oil
lamps at the Golden Temple
in Amritsar, India.*

5

Latoya Khoza, a dance student, gets ready to perform a classical Indian dance during a Diwali celebration in Durban, South Africa.

We have different customs.

All over the world,
we have different customs on
Diwali. But we all look forward
to it. It is the happiest of the
holidays!

We get ready for weeks. We
clean and decorate our homes.
Many of us buy new clothes,
and even gold jewelry.

*A girl plays with paper lanterns on
sale for Diwali in Bombay, India.*

*A boy in Uttar Pradesh, India,
brings home marigolds to decorate
his house for Diwali.*

There are so many sweets!

Years ago, our grandmothers and great-grandmothers spent days and days making different kinds of sweets to eat on Diwali. Some people still work hard making *barfi, peda, laddoos, kulfi,* and other goodies. But today we can buy candies, puddings, cakes, cookies, and other desserts in bakeries and shops. There are so many sweets!

A woman buys Diwali sweets in Guwahati, India.

Here is the best part— we buy lots of fireworks! (Our parents make sure that we buy only safe ones.) There are millions and millions sold all over India. In America we buy sparklers and noisemakers when they are on sale for the Fourth of July. We save them until Diwali.

Boys shop for fireworks at a roadside stand in Bangalore, India.

Mohammad Hussain Sheikh makes fuses for fireworks at a small factory outside Ahmadabad, India.

Sumithrin David lights a sparkler at a Diwali party in Bethesda, Maryland.

We buy lots of fireworks!

This kolam in Kuala Lumpur, Malaysia, is made from colored rice flour beads.

We make designs with rice flour.

The day before Diwali, we dust and sweep and polish every inch of our houses. We even whitewash our walls. Some people paint beautiful designs on the walls, too.

Girls in the Gujarat region of India decorate a house for Diwali.

We make designs with rice flour on the ground outside our homes. In South India we make small designs every day, but on Diwali we make large ones. In North India the rice designs are called *rangoli*, and in the South *kolam*.

And then it is time for Diwali to begin...

13

In South India we wake up very early in the morning. We take baths as if we were bathing in the holy River Ganga (Ganges). It is said that on Diwali the River Ganga is in all the waters of the world. On Diwali when we greet a friend we say, "Have you had your bath in the River Ganga?"

We rub warm oil onto our heads and wash it off. Then we dress in our new clothes.

Pilgrims bathe in the River Ganga during another Hindu festival called Kumbh Mela.

Have you had your bath?

A girl shows off her new clothes at a Diwali festival on Réunion, an island in the Indian Ocean.

We make as m[uch] noise as we can!

Just as dawn is breaking,

we set off our firecrackers.

We make as much noise as we can!
Our fireworks remind us of the
sounds of the battle long, long ago,
when good triumphed over evil.

*Children twirl Diwali sparklers
outside their lit-up homes in
Kathmandu, Nepal.*

A woman sells small statues of Lakshmi, the Hindu goddess of wealth, in Allahabad, India.

17th-century hanging lamp showing Lakshmi with two elephants

In North India, we celebrate

in the evening. We do a *puja,* or worship, to Lakshmi, at home or at a temple. Then we light special oil lamps called *deepa* all around the house. We string lights outside, too. Diwali is from the Sanskrit word *deepavali,* which means necklace of lights. The lights help Lakshmi find her way to our homes and give us good fortune.

We also set off firecrackers and light sparklers. Sometimes we go to big fireworks shows.

We light special oil lamps.

Indian girls place deepa on the Yamuna River behind the famous Taj Mahal, which is actually a Muslim mausoleum.

In part of India, Diwali marks the New Year. For some companies it is the start of the new business year.

People from the Punjab region of India gamble on Diwali. We are not allowed to gamble all year, but on Diwali we play card games for money. Some people even consider it bad luck not to gamble!

In some areas in northern India, the day after Diwali we make an offering of food to the god Krishna. We place 108 kinds of food on a pyramid of steps. For many different reasons 108 is a sacred number in Hinduism.

This new computer hard drive is part of a Diwali worship in Matthews, North Carolina, celebrating the start of a new business year.

We make an offering of food.

The offering of 108 different kinds of food is called annakut. *The sweet foods are placed at the top, closest to Krishna.*

A Diwali greeting card, with the elephant-headed god Ganesh, the god of blessings and one who removes obstacles.

For some of us, Diwali is a special time for brothers and sisters. Brothers visit sisters to honor them. Sisters cook for brothers.

For everyone it is a time to celebrate. We visit family and friends and bring sweets. Lots of sweets! Sometimes we eat too much. We take a homemade medicine called *lehyam* to make us feel better.

Because we can't always visit our family and friends in person, we send Diwali cards in the mail, and on the Internet.

We visit family and friends.

Three generations of a
South Indian family in
Chennai (formerly Madras)
celebrate Diwali together.

Diwali is the happiest festival.

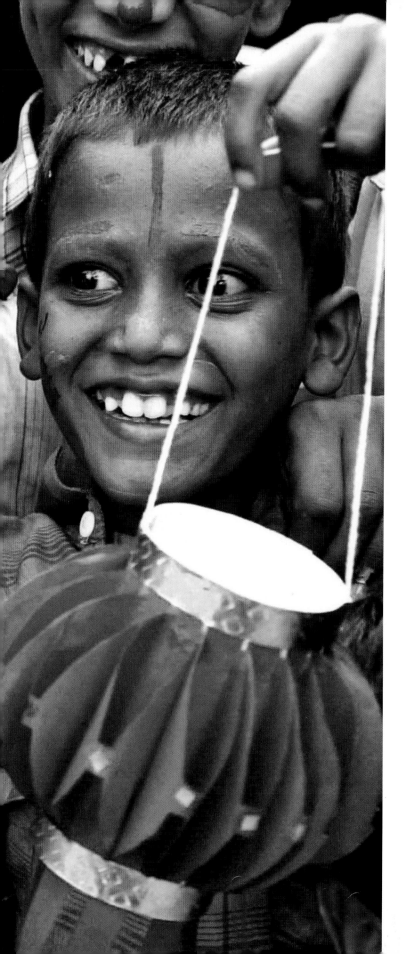

On Diwali we have new beginnings. We celebrate the victory of good over evil, of light over darkness. We spread that light all over the Earth. Diwali is the happiest festival.

Children in Bombay, India, celebrate Diwali with painted faces at a street fair.

MORE ABOUT DIWALI

Contents

Just the Facts	26
Glossary	26
Vasu's Peda	27
Play Teen Pathi!	28
Find Out More	29
Maps	30
Note from Dr. Vasudha Narayanan	31

Just the Facts

WHO CELEBRATES IT: Hindus, Sikhs, and Jains

WHAT: It is a holiday to celebrate the triumph of good over evil and light over darkness. It is also a holiday to welcome Lakshmi, the goddess of good fortune. In parts of North India, it is the New Year. Sikhs celebrate the return of one of their favorite gurus from captivity. Jains honor their teacher Mahavira, who gave his last teachings at this time.

WHEN: On a new moon day in October or November.

HOW LONG: In India and some other countries, Diwali is celebrated for two to five days. In the rest of the world, it is usually celebrated for one day.

ALSO KNOWN AS: Deepavali in South India, Deva Diwali by Jains; Bandi Chhorh Divas by Sikhs.

RITUAL: Many people do a *puja* (worship) to Lakshmi. Others take a ritual bath, symbolically bathing in the River Ganga. Lighting oil lamps, setting off fireworks, and decorating homes with lights are also important parts of the holiday.

FOOD: Sweets of many kinds.

Glossary

Deepa (DEE-puh): small oil lamps, usually made out of clay or earthenware. Also called *deepam* or *diya* (DEE-yuh).

Hindu (HIN-doo): a member of Hinduism, the major religion in India. Hindus believe that God comes to Earth as different creatures and people and in different shapes. Hindus from different areas have different practices and customs.

Jain (JINE): a member of a religion started in India in the sixth century B.C. Jains are concerned with the welfare of all beings on Earth.

Krishna (KRISH-nuh): one of the human forms of the god Vishnu.

Lakshmi (LOCK-shmee): the Hindu goddess of wealth, prosperity, and good fortune.

Puja (POO-juh): a worship ceremony.

Rama (RAH-mah): a human form of Vishnu; he was the king of Arodhya. Rama is everything that a good man should be. His story is told in the epic poem *The Ramayana*.

Sanskrit (SAN-skrit): an ancient language of India. Epics, hymns, and scripture are written in Sanskrit. A lot of English words have Sanskrit roots.

Sikh (SEEK): a member of a religion that was started in India in the early 16th century. Sikhs believe in one god. They must wear certain items of clothing. For example, men wear turbans.

Sita (SEE-tuh): Rama's wife. She is everything a good woman should be.

Vasu's Peda

By Vasudha Narayanan

This is an easy sweet to make for Diwali.

INGREDIENTS:
1 stick butter
1 can (14 oz.) sweetened condensed milk
1 ½ cups milk powder
¼ teaspoon cardamom powder (optional)

Vasudha Narayanan's peda

YOU WILL ALSO NEED:
1 plastic spool of thread, with the end paper ripped off to reveal a hole with triangles around it.

1. Let butter sit at room temperature for about one hour.

2. Mix butter and sweetened condensed milk.

3. Microwave until the mixture bubbles.

4. Add milk powder, stir, and cook for 1 minute.

5. Stir and cook for 1 minute increments until the consistency is thick and doughy (may take about 6-8 minutes).

6. Stir in cardamom powder if you like.

7. Make small balls and flatten them lightly. (If it is sticky, you can rub your palms with melted butter.)

8. Press down the end of the spool of thread to make a decorative pattern.

9. Let cool. Enjoy!

Makes about two dozen peda. Store any leftovers in an airtight container.

A worker at the Biggest Sweet Shop of Shillong, India, checks a large display of Diwali sweets.

Play Teen Pathi!

Teen Pathi is a gambling card game that is played on Diwali. Gambling on Diwali is supposed to bring good luck and good fortune from Lakshmi. Here is a version for kids.

NUMBER OF PLAYERS: **3 or more**
WHAT YOU NEED:
- **A regular deck of cards**
- **Game pieces: You can use pennies, nuts, raisins, chocolate candy, toothpicks, or whatever you want. You use these to bet. Use about ten game pieces per person.**

TO START: Each player gets the same number of game pieces. One player starts as the dealer. Deal each player three cards facedown. At first, nobody looks at his or her cards.

Take turns going around in a circle from the dealer. When it's your turn, you may look at your cards or not. If you do not look at your cards, put one piece in the center. That is your bet to remain in the round.

If you do look at your cards, you may choose to fold (stop playing). If you want to continue, you have to put in two pieces. To decide whether to continue or fold, you have to guess whether your cards are better than everyone else's cards. If you think other people can beat you, you should fold. (See right for the rank of hands.)

You can stay "blind" for the whole round. If you are "blind," you have to put in only one piece to stay in the round. But you can choose to look at your cards at any point. If you look at your cards, you have to put in two pieces to stay in the

game. If you don't want to stay in, you fold. Keep going around in the circle until two people have folded. If everyone folds except one person, that person wins without having to show his or her cards. If two people stay in, then they show their cards and the best hand wins. (If you find that you are going around too many times and using up your game pieces too quickly, limit the number of times you can go around.)

RANK OF HANDS:
Best hand: **Three of a kind. The higher the cards the better. Ace is high. So three aces beats three fives, etc.**

Second best hand: **Two of a kind, or a pair. The highest pair wins. If two people have the same pair (6 and 6), then the person with the highest third card wins. (So 6, 6, King beats 6, 6, 10.)**

Third best hand: **High card. If no one has three of a kind or a pair, the person with the highest card wins. If two people have the same high card, then use the second-highest card as a tiebreaker.**

The winner takes all the pieces that were put in the center. If two people both have exactly the same winning hand, they each take half.

For the next round, the person to the left of the dealer becomes the dealer, and deals out three cards to each player. Keep playing rounds until one person wins all the pieces.

Find Out More

BOOKS

Those with a star (*) are especially good for children. Remember when you are looking for books or other sources about Diwali that it is also spelled in different ways, such as Divali and Divaali. It is also called Deepavali.

* Kalman, Bobbie. *India: The Culture.* Crabtree Publishing Company, 2001. This is a good book with lots of information about India. It is in the Lands, Peoples, and Cultures Series. You might also want to look at *India: The People* and *India: The Land*. Ages 9-12.

* MacMillan, Dianne M. *Diwali: Hindu Festival of Lights.* Enslow, 1997. This is a really good book that goes into detail about all aspects of Diwali, including stories of Rama and Krishna. It also gives good background information on Hinduism.

Singh, Chitralekha and Prem Nath. *Hindu Festivals, Fairs and Fasts.* Crest Publishing House, 2002. A comprehensive book published in India.

Singh, Chitralekha and Prem Nath. *Lakshmi.* Crest Publishing House, 2002. A book about all aspects of Lakshmi, with a chapter on Diwali.

* Verma, Jatinder. *The Story of Divaali.* Illustrated by Nilesh Mistry. Barefoot Books, 2002. This is a retelling for children of the epic poem *The Ramayana*, especially as it relates to Diwali. It's a great story!

WEB SITES

http://www.diwalifestival.org/
An excellent Web site about Diwali, with many pages and lots of things to read and do.

http://www.activityvillage.co.uk/diwali.htm
This is a site that is especially for children. It has information about Diwali, crafts to do, and links to other good pages. Highly recommended.

http://www.diwalimela.com/aroundtheworld/
This page tells about how Diwali is celebrated around the world. It is part of a Web site where you can see all kinds of Diwali gifts to buy.

http://www.theholidayspot.com/diwali/
A great site all about Diwali. You can get information, send a Diwali greeting card by e-mail, and even get Diwali wallpaper for your computer.

http://www.indoindians.com/festival/diwali3.htm
This Web page has many recipes for sweets to make on Diwali. They call for traditional Indian ingredients.

http://news.bbc.co.uk/cbbcnews/hi/club/your_reports/newsid_1677000/1677032.stm
A ten-year-old girl tells how she celebrates Diwali.

http://en.wikipedia.org/wiki/Diwali
An article on Diwali in Wikipedia, the free online encyclopedia. With links to other articles on subjects such as Sanskrit, India, and Hindu.

Lighting Up the Map

Two photographs taken by a satellite on two nights in November 2004 show how much light in India was visible from space during and after Diwali. Compare the two images to see how the lights and fireworks that people used on Diwali lit up the country. The map, right, shows India (in white) and the other nations (in gray) where the photographs in this book were taken.

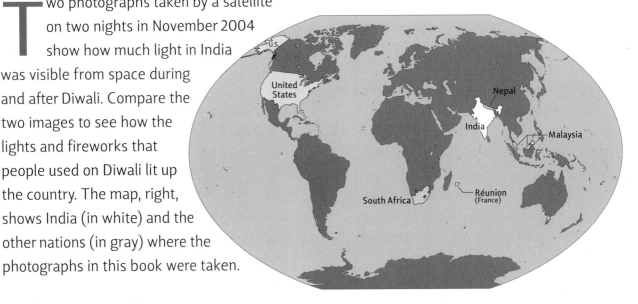

India During Diwali

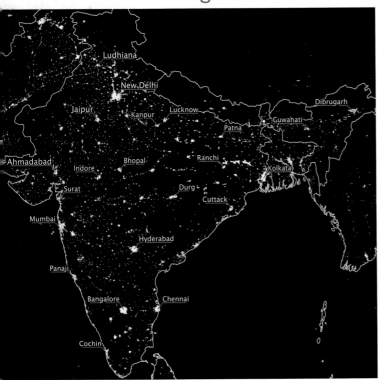

India Six Days After Diwali

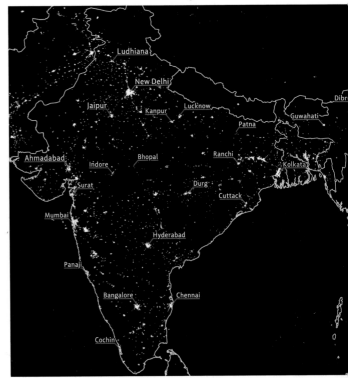

Diwali: A Holiday of Goodness & Light
by Dr. Vasudha Narayanan

Among the many days of feasting and fasting on the Hindu calendar, Diwali—or Deepavali*, as South Indians like me call it—is one of the most important and joyous holidays of the year.

Hindus have rich and diverse traditions, and people from various parts of India connect Deepavali with different narratives. Most Hindus do not think one story is real and the others are wrong; like many other Hindu concepts and festivals, we think of Deepavali as having multiple narratives and meanings.

All the stories associated with Deepavali, however, speak of the joy connected with the victory of light over darkness, knowledge over ignorance, and goodness over evil. Since the time of the Upanishads (part of the Vedas, the earliest holy texts of the Hindus), darkness is connected with ignorance, untruth, and death.

Most Hindus, though not all, think of Vishnu as the Supreme Being who creates, protects, and eventually destroys the universe. This cycle of creation and destruction is repeated again and again. Within these enormous cycles of time, sometimes lasting billions of years, Vishnu comes to Earth in various forms. Many Hindus believe that he does so to rid the Earth of evil. Deepavali is associated with many of these incarnations of Vishnu: as Krishna, Rama, and to some as Trivikrama.

Most people from the south of India celebrate the victory of Krishna over a demon called Narakasura ("the demon of hell"). Some Hindus believe that Krishna and his wife Satyabhama won the war over this demon just as dawn was breaking. During the celebration of Deepavali, people set off fireworks at home anytime after 3 a.m. As the light of the fireworks, and then dawn, overcomes the darkness, we think of Krishna's victory.

In many parts of northern India, Hindus may never have heard of this particular story of Krishna. Instead, they celebrate Deepavali as the day when Rama returned from exile to his capital, Ajodhya, after he defeated a demon called Ravana. This story is told in the famous epic *The Ramayana*.

A lesser known story, which some Hindus from the state of Kerala in India associate with Deepavali, is that of King Bali. Vishnu was incarnated as a colossal being called Trivikrama and strode over the Earth and heavens. In this story, Bali is said to have pride and arrogance and ultimately surrenders himself to Trivikrama, who grants him salvation. People in Kerala think that on Deepavali, Bali visits the world to see it so joyfully lit up.

In some parts of India, Lakshmi, the goddess of good fortune, is said to come home on this day and grace those houses that are lit up in her honor. For some businesses Deepavali signals the beginning of the fiscal year.

During Deepavali one spends time with family and friends. Most people in India celebrate Deepavali at home, in front yards, and in the streets right outside their homes. However, Hindus who live in other countries have community celebrations in temple halls and auditoriums. In the diaspora people from different parts of India share their stories and customs.

In India and many other countries, new clothes, a plethora of sweets and snacks, good food, and traditions of giving gifts have made Deepavali a domestic and community celebration as well as a commercially profitable time for shopkeepers and businesses.

No matter which narratives Hindus associate with Diwali and which customs they practice, it is always a happy, joyous holiday filled with light, with family and friends, and with goodness.

Vasudha Narayanan is a professor of religion and the director of the Center for the Study of Hindu Traditions (CHiTra) at the University of Florida in Gainesville.

---

* The word Diwali is a shortening of Deepavali, which comes from the Sanskrit *deepa*, meaning light and *vali*, meaning row. We in South India use and prefer the original word.

PICTURE CREDITS

Front Cover © AFP/Getty Images; Back Cover © Lindsay Hebberd/ Corbis; page 1 © Lynsey Addario/Corbis; page 2 © Indranil Mukherjee/AFP/Getty Images; page 3 © Corbis; pages 4-5 © Aman Sharma/AP Wide World Photos; page 6 © Rajesh Jantilal/AFP/ Getty Images; page 7 (top) © Sebastian D'Souza/AFP/Getty Images; (bottom) © Greg Elms/Lonely Planet Images; pages 8-9 © Subhamoy Bhattacharjee; page 10 (top) © Indranil Mukherjee/ AFP/Getty Images; (bottom) © AFP/Getty Images; page 11 © Lori Epstein; page 12 © Bazuki Muhammad/Reuters/Corbis; page 13 © Lindsay Hebbard/Corbis; page 14 © Chris Hellier/Corbis; page 15 © Lynsey Addario/Corbis; pages 16-17 © Joe Viesti; page 18 (top) © Rajesh Kumar Singh/AP Wide World Photos; (bottom) © Angelo Hornak /Corbis; page 19 © Brijesh Singh/Reuters/Corbis; pages 20 & 21 © BAPS Swaminarayan Sanstha; page 22 © Barnabas Kindersley/ Dorling Kindersley; page 23 © Shoba Narayan; pages 24-25 © Rajesh Nirgude/AP Wide World Photos; page 27 (top) © Deborah Heiligman; (bottom) © Subhamoy Bhattacharjee; page 30 (both) National Remote Sensing Agency, India.

Text copyright © 2006 Deborah Heiligman
First paperback printing 2008
ISBN: 978-1-4263-0291-6

Library of Congress Cataloging-in-Publication Data
Heiligman, Deborah.
Celebrate Diwali/Deborah Heiligman; consultant, Dr. Vasudha Narayanan.
    p. cm. — (Holidays around the world)
ISBN 0-7922-5922-X (hardcover) — ISBN 0-7922-5923-8 (library binding)
1. Divali—Juvenile literature. I. Narayanan, Vasudha. II. Title. III. Holidays around the world (National Geographic Society (U.S.))
BL1239.82.D58H45 2006
294.5'36 — dc22
                          2006003426

ISBN 10: 0-7922-5922-X (hardcover) — ISBN 10: 0-7922-5923-8 (library binding) — ISBN 13: 978-0-7922-5922-0 (hardcover) — ISBN 13: 978-0-7922-5923-7 (library binding)

FRONT COVER: A family in Calcutta, India, lights fireworks as part of a Diwali celebration in 1999. BACK COVER: A girl in Saputara, India, shows off her Diwali handiwork, a wall decorated with drawings and handprints.

For Barbara Kerley, who knows why

ACKNOWLEDGMENTS

Many, many thanks to Sreenath Sreenivasan, who helped me with this book in so many ways. Thanks also to Professor John Hawley, of Barnard, and to Pamela Persaud. Thanks to all the people who sent in recipes for Diwali sweets. We couldn't use them all, but my family enjoyed many of them and so they thank you, too! An "I owe you" goes to Aaron Weiner, game master, who helped me create this version of Teen Pathi. And many thanks to Gail Gorgol, librarian at Churchville Elementary School, and Nancy Sandberg, fourth grade teacher at Buckingham Friends school, who asked their children to play the game. Thank you to those who played it: Shane Brown, Juliana Mangin, Emily Rucker, Josh Breidinger, Steve Blackman, Anna Ebert, Jenni McGuire, Jake Gross, Aditi Patil, Matt Berger, Taylor Dillon, Shane Magrann, Scarlett Waldman, Blake Rivas, and Katie Rintala.

One of the world's largest nonprofit scientific and educational organizations, the National Geographic Society was founded in 1888 "for the increase and diffusion of geographic knowledge." Fulfilling this mission, the Society educates and inspires millions every day through its magazines, books, television programs, videos, maps and atlases, research grants, the National Geographic Bee, teacher workshops, and innovative classroom materials. The Society is supported through membership dues, charitable gifts, and income from the sale of its educational products. This support is vital to National Geographic's mission to increase global understanding and promote conservation of our planet through exploration, research, and education. For more information, please call 1-800-NGS-LINE (647-5463) or write to the following address:

NATIONAL GEOGRAPHIC SOCIETY
1145 17th Street N.W.
Washington, D.C. 20036-4688 U.S.A.
Visit the Society's Web site at www.nationalgeographic.com

John M. Fahey, Jr., *President and Chief Executive Officer*
Gilbert M. Grosvenor, *Chairman of the Board*
Nina D. Hoffman, *Executive Vice President, President of Books & Education Publishing Group*
Stephen Mico, *Executive Vice President, Children's Books & Education Publishing Group*
Bea Jackson, *Design Director, Children's Books & Education Publishing Group*
Margaret Sidlosky, *Illustrations Director, Children's Books & Education Publishing Group*

STAFF FOR THIS BOOK

Nancy Laties Feresten, *Vice President, Editor-in-Chief of Children's Books*
Jennifer Emmett, Sue Macy, *Project Editors*
Jim Hiscott, *Art Director*
Lori Epstein, *Illustrations Editor*
Carl Mehler, *Director of Maps*
Priyanka Lamichhane, *Editorial Assistant*
Rebecca Hinds, *Managing Editor*
R. Gary Colbert, *Production Director*
Lewis R. Bassford, *Production Manager*
Vincent P. Ryan, Maryclare Tracy, *Manufacturing Managers*

Book design is by 3+Co.
The body text in the book is set in Mrs. Eaves.
The display text is in Lisboa.